E.
BOOK SERIES

Eat Like a Local- Sarasota: Sarasota Florida Food Guide

I have lived in the Sarasota area since 1998 and learned about many great places that I want to try. –Conoal

EAT LIKE A LOCAL-CONNECTICUT: Connecticut Food Guide

This a great guide to try different places in Connecticut to eat. Can't wait to try them all! The author is awesome to explore and try all these different foods/drinks. There are places I didn't know they existed until I got this book and I am a CT resident myself! –Caroline J. H.

EAT LIKE A LOCAL- LAS VEGAS: Las Vegas Nevada Food Guide

Perfect food guide for any tourist traveling to Vegas or any local looking to go outside their comfort zone! –TheBondes

Eat Like a Local-Jacksonville: Jacksonville Florida Food Guide

Loved the recommendations. Great book from someone who knows their way around Jacksonville. –Anonymous

EAT LIKE A LOCAL- COSTA BRAVA: Costa Brava Spain Food Guide

The book was very well written. Visited a few of the restaurants in the book, they were great! Sylvia V.

Eat Like a Local-Sacramento: Sacramento California Food Guide

As a native of Sacramento, Emerald's book touches on some of our areas premier spots for food and fun. She skims the surface of what Sacramento has to offer recommending locations in historical, popular areas where even more jewels can be found. –Katherine G.

EAT LIKE A LOCAL- PARIS

Paris France Food Guide

Mackenzie Leighton

Eat Like a Local Paris- Copyright © 2021 by CZYK Publishing LLC. All Rights Reserved.

All rights reserved. No part of this book may be reproduced in any form or by any electronic or mechanical means including information storage and retrieval systems, without permission in writing from the author. The only exception is by a reviewer, who may quote short excerpts in a review.

The statements in this book are of the authors and may not be the views of CZYK Publishing.

Cover designed by: Lisa Rusczyk Ed. D.

CZYK Publishing Since 2011.
CZYKPublishing.com
Eat Like a Local

Lock Haven, PA
All rights reserved.
ISBN: 9798428442656

BOOK DESCRIPTION

Are you excited about planning your next trip? Do you want an edible experience? Would you like some culinary guidance from a local? If you answered yes to any of these questions, then this Eat Like a Local book is for you. Eat Like a Local - Paris by Mackenzie Leighton offers the inside scoop on food and culinary culture in Paris. Culinary tourism is an important aspect of any travel experience. Food has the ability to tell you a story of a destination, its landscapes, and culture on a single plate. Most food guides tell you how to eat like a tourist. Although there is nothing wrong with that, as part of the Eat Like a Local series, this book will give you a food guide from someone who has lived at your next culinary destination.

In these pages, you will discover advice on having a unique edible experience. This book will not tell you exact addresses or hours but instead will give you excitement and knowledge of food and drinks from a local that you may not find in other travel food guides.

Eat like a local. Slow down, stay in one place, and get to know the food, people, and culture. By the time you finish this book, you will be eager and prepared to travel to your next culinary destination.

OUR STORY

Traveling has always been a passion of the creator of the Eat Like a Local book series. During Lisa's travels in Malta, instead of tasting what the city offered, she ate at a large fast-food chain. However, she realized that her traveling experience would have been more fulfilling if she had experienced the best of local cuisines. Most would agree that food is one of the most important aspects of a culture. Through her travels, Lisa learned how much locals had to share with tourists, especially about food. Lisa created the Eat Like a Local book series to help connect people with locals which she discovered is a topic that locals are very passionate about sharing. So please join me and: Eat, drink, and explore like a local.

TABLE OF CONTENTS

Eat Like a Local-
Book Series Reviews
BOOK DESCRIPTION
OUR STORY
TABLE OF CONTENTS
DEDICATION
ABOUT THE AUTHOR
HOW TO USE THIS BOOK
FROM THE PUBLISHER
1. Start Your Morning Off The Right Way
2. Butter, Butter, and More Butter
3. The Difference Between a Boulangerie and a Pâtisserie
4. A Box of French Pastries
5. The Best Gluten-Free Bakeries
6. Let's Talk About Baguettes
7. The Best Sourdough in the City
8. Everything You Need To Know About Macarons
9. Meal Times and Importance
10. Snack Time Is For Everyone
11. The Best Time of The Day: Apero
12. Terrasse Culture: Rain or Shine
13. Eating On The Go is a No-No
14. Take-Out and Delivery Options

15. The Difference Between a Crepe and a Galette
16. La Rue de Montparnasse: Crêpes and Galettes Galore
17. Got a Train to Catch? Get a Crêpe to Go
18. Tourist Traps: Areas To Be Weary Of
19. Why Do The Servers Hate Us?
20. Tips: Are They Expected?
21. Les Bouillons: Traditional French Food On a Budget
22. Date Night in Belleville: Drinks and Dumplings
23. The Main Parisian Chinatown
24. Little Tokyo: The Japanese Quarter on the Rue Sainte-Anne
25. Michelin Star Restaurants: Treat Yourself to Culinary Excellence
26. Put Your Taste Buds To The Test
27. Big Mamma: Traditional Italian Trattorias
28. La Felicita: An Italian Food Market and Nightlife Hotspot
29. Ground Control: Eclectic Food Hall
30. Take a Stroll Through a Farmer's Market
31. Let's Talk About Cheese
32. The Proper Order For Cheese Tasting
33. The Best Part About The Holidays
34. A January Tradition: Galettes Des Rois

35. La Fête De La Chandeleur: Celebrate With Crêpes
36. Wine and Street Food in Montmartre: Fête Des Vendanges
37. Late Night Eats
38. The Best Falafel in Paris
39. How Do You Like Your Meat?
40. Certain Meats Can Be Rosé and They Should Be
41. Culinary Faux-Pas: What To Be Careful Of
42. Simplicity, Simplicity, Simplicity
43. The Best Spots For Mexican Food
44. Mosquée de Paris: Tagines, Pastries and Mint Tea
45. A Meal On The House
46. Taste the Famous Ice Cream at Berthillon
47. Where To Make Reservations and Find New Insider Hotspots
48. Best Burger Joints
49. Artisanal Coffee Roasters
50. Let Your Taste Buds Lead The Way

BONUS TIPS

51. The Best Cocktail Bars in Paris
52. Did Someone Say Speakeasy?
53. Take In the Views On a Rooftop Bar
54. Where To Listen To Live Jazz
55. The Hotspots for Pop, Rock, and Indie Concerts

56. Museum Must-Sees
57. Hidden Treasures
58. Stroll Through Monet's Gardens in Giverny
59. Get Off The Beaten Path To The Medieval Town Of Provins
60. Live Like The King and Queen For a Day in Versailles

Other Resources:

READ OTHER BOOKS BY

CZYK PUBLISHING

DEDICATION

This book is dedicated to my father, Jeffrey Leighton, who taught me how to appreciate good food and continues to inspire me with his creativity in the kitchen.

ABOUT THE AUTHOR

Mackenzie Leighton is a writer, musician, and florist who lives in Paris, France. Originally from Maine in the Northeastern United States, she studied social justice and arts activism at New York University and then moved to Paris upon graduating in 2017. She spends her time playing concerts with her band, crafting bouquets for clients, and traveling around Europe to get inspiration for her future albums.

As an expat that is very integrated in the Parisian scene, Mackenzie has cultivated a handful of local tips, particularly when it comes to food. She grew up in a home where dinner was an important time of the day where the whole family could come together and appreciate a good meal and good company. Her parents also instilled in her a strong sense of curiosity for discovering other cultures, as her first trip to Paris was at the young age of five.

As her partner is French, she now has been immersed in the culture and customs of dining in a French family and has seen how they differ from her American upbringing. She hopes to share this knowledge with her readers, hoping to inspire others to discover new food and cultures in the process.

HOW TO USE THIS BOOK

The goal of this book is to help culinary travelers either dream or experience different edible experiences by providing opinions from a local. The author has made suggestions based on their own knowledge. Please do your own research before traveling to the area in case the suggested locations are unavailable.

Travel Advisories: As a first step in planning any trip abroad, check the Travel Advisories for your intended destination.
https://travel.state.gov/content/travel/en/traveladvisories/traveladvisories.html

FROM THE PUBLISHER

Traveling can be one of the most important parts of a person's life. The anticipation and memories that you have are some of the best. As a publisher of the *Eat Like a Local*, Greater Than a Tourist, as well as the popular *50 Things to Know* book series, we strive to help you learn about new places, spark your imagination, and inspire you. Wherever you are and whatever you do I wish you safe, fun, and inspiring travel.

Lisa Rusczyk Ed. D.
CZYK Publishing

Eat Like a Local

"If you are lucky enough to have lived in Paris as a young man, then wherever you go for the rest of your life, it stays with you, for all of Paris is a moveable feast."

-Ernest Hemingway

France is known around the world for its fine attention to detail in the culinary arts. When we think of the cliches surrounding French culture, we think first and foremost about food- fresh produce, delicious artisanal cheeses, and fine wine. Though Lyon is technically the gastronomic capital of the world, Paris is not too far behind. Just the offer alone is astounding; according to the World Cities Culture Forum, in 2017 Paris was home to 44,896 different restaurants. In 2020, 119 of these restaurants had one or more Michelin stars. For the real gourmands out there, Paris is a haven of fine dining and culinary exception.

For those who enjoy good quality food and have a budget, this city has equally lots to offer. Paris is after all, a cosmopolitan hub where cultures intertwine. One of the things I love about Paris is that you really can have it all when it comes to food. One can enjoy a traditional French meal in the Marais and the next day enjoy authentic Chinese dumplings in Belleville. There really is something for everyone. However, endless options can also be a challenge in itself and you may find yourself struggling on where to even begin. There are so many delicious dishes to choose from!

I hope these tips will help you narrow down what you are looking for in the Paris food scene and will inspire you to try something new. I've had mostly positive experiences while dining in Paris, and I've learned from the times where my lack of knowledge about culinary culture in France got the best of me. With time and experience you can eat like a local too!

From where to find the best croissants to dining etiquette, I've learned these insider tips firsthand and hope they will point you in the right direction. It will then be up to you to set off on your own Parisian food adventure!

Eat Like a Local

Paris
France

Eat Like a Local

Paris France Climate

	High	Low
January	46	37
February	48	37
March	55	42
April	62	46
May	68	52
June	74	57
July	78	61
August	78	60
September	71	55
October	63	50
November	52	43
December	47	39

GreaterThanaTourist.com

Temperatures are in Fahrenheit degrees.
Source: NOAA

Eat Like a Local

1. START YOUR MORNING OFF THE RIGHT WAY

What's the first thing any Parisian does when they wake up in the morning? Besides maybe smoking a cigarette, as Parisians are known to do, they go to their local boulangerie (bakery) to get some fresh croissants or perhaps a pain au chocolat. With over 30,000 boulangeries in Paris, there is usually one within a five minute walk from anywhere in the city. I have at least three boulangeries next to my apartment and I did what any good Parisian would do- try them all and compare!

Some notable boulangeries that are hotspots among locals include Du Pain et des Idées in the 10th arrondissement and The French Bastards in the 11th and 2nd.

2. BUTTER, BUTTER, AND MORE BUTTER

Butter is an important staple of French cuisine, and particularly, French pastries. French butter is known around the world as particularly delicious, most likely due to its higher fat content and how it is made. Before living in France, I wouldn't think of having just bread and butter as a snack in itself and now I seem to do this almost daily. When the butter is salty and rich and the baguette has just come out of the bakery oven, that's all you need.

When choosing your morning croissant, there are two different types to choose from: the croissant "ordinaire" (ordinary) and the croissant "au beurre" (butter). Make sure you order the croissant "au beurre"- it's the real deal.

3. THE DIFFERENCE BETWEEN A BOULANGERIE AND A PÂTISSERIE

If you ask a baker, the difference between a Boulangerie (bakery) and a Pâtisserie (pastry shop) lies in the process of fermentation. The boulanger (baker) works primarily with dough that has been fermented to create not only baguettes but also croissants and other morning treats. In simpler terms, the patissier (pastry chef) works with everything that is sweet: cakes, tartes, and other delicious French treats that I will introduce you to in the next tip.

You will often find pastries in a bakery and you can sometimes find bread in a pastry shop. The two domains often go hand in hand, which gives us the hybrid "Boulangerie Pâtisserie" where you can have the best of both worlds.

4. A BOX OF FRENCH PASTRIES

If you want to try an assortment of French pastries, it is custom to go to a pâtisserie and pick out various treats to take away. I will often do this if I've been invited to dinner at a friend's house and asked to bring dessert. It's the perfect way to try different pastries and flavors. Among the classics and my favorites are the small tartes au citron (lemon tartes), éclairs, and mille-feuille. When it comes to french pastries, expect a lot of cream and butter.

5. THE BEST GLUTEN-FREE BAKERIES

For those who are gluten-free, Paris may seem like a difficult place to navigate. Despite the bread centric culture, there are options for you as well! Two places to check out include Boulangerie Chambelland in the 11th and Biosphère Café in the 8th. My personal favorite that gets as close to the real thing without using gluten is Noglu with two locations in the 7th and 11th.

6. LET'S TALK ABOUT BAGUETTES

Like many aspects of French food, there is nuance: one seemingly simple product can have subtle differences. Baguettes fall into this category. From an outsider point of view, a baguette is a baguette. From the French perspective, there are multiple kinds of baguettes that vary in composition and form.

There is the standard baguette that is quite white on the inside and has a lighter texture. My personal favorite and that of many Parisians is the baguette "tradition" which is more rustic with a crunchier crust. Certain "pains spéciaux" or "special breads" will include baguettes with nuts, seeds, or multiple grains in them. The baguette "en épi" is definitely the most eye-catching one as it is shaped like a stalk of wheat with the bread alternating sides. Why not try them all?

7. THE BEST SOURDOUGH IN THE CITY

If you're looking to expand your horizons beyond baguettes, look no further than the historical Parisian bakery of Maison Poilâne. With four different locations across the city, they are the go-to place to find the best sourdough loaves that Paris has to offer. You can also find their bread in most supermarkets like Monoprix and Franprix.

The bakery began in 1932 and uses stone-ground flour, natural fermentation, and a wood-fired oven to bake round sourdough loaves. They continue to use traditional methods and are internationally known in the bread world.

8. EVERYTHING YOU NEED TO KNOW ABOUT MACARONS

When you think of Paris, those small colorful macarons probably come to mind! Though macarons are now widely seen as a French delicacy, many believe that they were actually brought over from Italy by Queen Catherine de Medici and her pastry chefs in the 1500s. Macarons are a sweet meringue-based cookie made with egg white, granulated sugar, icing sugar, almond meal, and food coloring. They are filled with chocolate ganache, buttercream, or jam, and they come in many flavors. The most traditional flavors are chocolate, vanilla, pistachio, coffee, and strawberry.

You can find macarons in almost every patisserie in the city, but the two most famous spots known for their delicious macarons are Ladurée and Pierre Hermé. Ladurée has more of the traditional flavors and Pierre Hermé tends to experiment more with flavors, but both are exquisite!

9. MEAL TIMES AND IMPORTANCE

In France, there are three main meals throughout the day with a snack time called "le goûter" in the late afternoon that I'll get to in the next tip. Breakfast, or "le petit déjeuner" is usually simple and light, with either some yogurt and muesli, a soft boiled egg with toast, or a croissant and piece of fruit. Compared to an American or English breakfast complete with eggs and pancakes, the French prefer to keep it light and healthy. Nonetheless, brunch is starting to become more popular on the weekends, and there are hotspots popping up all around the city to enjoy a late morning meal amongst friends.

Lunch, or "le déjeuner", is usually anytime between 12pm and 3pm and can last a good hour or two depending on the context. Most restaurants will close around 3pm for a couple hours before opening up again later around 6pm or 7pm for their dinner service. Many places offer "formules" or lunch menus where you pay a fixed price to get an "entrée + plat + dessert", or appetizer + main dish + dessert.

There is a cliché that dinner in France starts late and can last for hours upon end. This can be true, but there are really no rules that prohibit you from eating dinner early. A usual dinner will start around 8pm and go until 9:30 or 10pm. Unlike what I like to call the "early bird special" that is common in American households of eating dinner around 5 or 6pm, the French are still finishing their late afternoon snack during this time or just starting pre dinner drinks, otherwise known as Apero.

10. SNACK TIME IS FOR EVERYONE

Snack time, or "le goûter", is an important part of the day around 4pm or 5pm where one can enjoy a savory or sweet snack. It usually includes bread or chocolate and some juice or a hot tea, and is just as common amongst adults as it is with children.

During my first year in Paris I worked as an au pair and became very familiar with this ritual. This small meal in between lunch and dinner is like the equivalent of a tea time in England, and usually coincides with children getting out of school. After picking up the children from school, we would often stop at the boulangerie to get some bread or a sweet snack to bring home or eat in the park.

11. THE BEST TIME OF THE DAY: APERO

The all important "Apero" is a key time of the day when working hours have ended and the night has just begun. Apero is the familiar way of saying "apéritif" which means a drink to open up the appetite and start the evening festivities. It is often an alcoholic beverage of sorts, whether that be a cocktail, a beer, or a glass of wine, and is accompanied by small snacks such as olives, chips, or nuts. Friends will get together at a bar or someone's apartment for apero before having dinner or going out on the town. Apero can be any night of the week or weekend, and when you do this among colleagues it is usually referred to as an "after work".

If you are invited to someone's home for an "apéro dinatoire", it means that apero and dinner are one in the same. Instead of having a sit-down meal, there will be different small plates to snack on throughout the evening. You will spend hours enjoying drinks, tapas, and conversation, and if you're still hungry later you can get some late-night eats on your way home (check out tip 37).

12. TERRASSE CULTURE: RAIN OR SHINE

In Paris, the "terrasse", or the outside seating of cafés, is a big part of daily life. No matter the season, people will enjoy a coffee or drink outside, rain or shine. I really appreciate this aspect of the city and the fact that Parisians take advantage of the outdoor space all year round. It is most likely because they are notorious for smoking, and the benefit of the terrasse is that you can smoke and enjoy your drink at the same time. It is also a great way to people-watch and be fully immersed in the vibrancy of the city.

Do people still sit outside on the terrasses in the winter? The answer is yes. The cafés usually have heat lamps installed on their terrasses so that you can stay warm even in the winter, enjoying a vin chaud or hot chocolate. Perhaps the reason for why the heated terrasses work so well is that Paris winters can be quite mild. It is often rainy but rarely snows and doesn't get as cold as it does in New York, for example. When I lived in New York, I never remember sitting outside at a restaurant or bar in the wintertime. It was never a part of the culture as it is in Paris.

13. EATING ON THE GO IS A NO-NO

When I lived in New York, it was not uncommon to eat on the go. If I was in a hurry, I would walk down the street while eating a sandwich for example. I didn't think much of it at the time but now I would feel very uncomfortable doing that, especially in Paris. There is no rule against eating on the go in France and you won't be stopped by the police or anything, but you may get some strange looks.

Paris is a fast moving city just like any other large metropole, but people always have time to sit down and eat. When there is so much importance placed on food and the culinary arts, the idea of fast food conflicts with these values. Of course fast food restaurants are common in Paris- you can find a Mcdonalds in every neighborhood- but the culture of eating on the go or in a hurry is less prevalent. Even if you just have 5 minutes, you can enjoy your meal on a park bench or in a chair in one of the many beautiful public gardens.

14. TAKE-OUT AND DELIVERY OPTIONS

Take-out and delivery options have become more popular since 2020, as all restaurants were forced to close during the pandemic and had to adapt. The most popular applications for ordering food in Paris are Uber Eats, Deliveroo, and Just Eat. Most restaurants also offer take-out options if they do not use one of these services, so don't hesitate to ask for your meal "à emporter", or to take away.

Do the French actually order take-out? I would say yes, but not nearly as much as Americans do. There is definitely a strong appreciation for a home cooked meal or going out to eat at a restaurant. In certain contexts however, when Parisians want to spend a cozy night in or have friends over for drinks, they may order up some pizzas to the apartment.

15. THE DIFFERENCE BETWEEN A CREPE AND A GALETTE

When one thinks of French food, crêpes probably come to mind. There is however a similar thin pancake called a galette that you also may have tried but maybe have not noticed the difference. Like many of the subtle differences in French cuisine, this is an important one to keep in mind so that you can eat like a local.

The main difference between crêpes and galettes is the flour: crêpes are made from wheat flour and galettes are made from buckwheat flour. The other main difference is that crêpes are usually accompanied with sweet ingredients such as butter and sugar or melted chocolate, and galettes are for the savory ingredients, such as ham, cheese, and an egg. Just remember: crêpe=sweet and galette=savory.

… Eat Like a Local

16. LA RUE DE MONTPARNASSE: CRÊPES AND GALETTES GALORE

If you're looking to eat crêpes and galettes in Paris, look no further than the Rue de Montparnasse that runs between the 6th and 14th arrondissements. More than a dozen creperies line this street as it is right next to the Montparnasse train station, where the trains run from Paris to Brittany. As galettes are a traditional dish from Brittany, it's only fitting that travelers coming to Paris from this region would be craving a meal from home.

So skip the line at the crêpe stand in front of the Eiffel Tower and head on over to the Rue de Montparnasse for a more authentic experience. If you really want the full package, you can have a galette as a savory main dish, a sweet crêpe as a dessert, and a bowl of cider to accompany your meal. A classic galette and one of my personal favorites is the galette "complète" with ham, cheese, and a sunny side up egg. If you're feeling a bit more adventurous, you can try a traditional galette with andouille, a smoked pork sausage made from pig's intestines.

17. GOT A TRAIN TO CATCH? GET A CRÊPE TO GO

Don't have time to sit down for a full meal at one of the crêperies? Across from the Edgar Quintet metro station on the corner of the Rue de Montparnasse is a little crêpe and sandwich window at the Café de la Place. When I worked in the area, my colleagues and I would often enjoy these crêpes or sandwiches to go and eat in one of the "squares", otherwise known as small parks, nearby. It's one of those establishments in Paris that seems like it's been there forever, catering to the locals of the neighborhood. I personally love their paninis!

18. TOURIST TRAPS: AREAS TO BE WEARY OF

As Paris is one of the top destinations for tourists in the world, there are many areas and restaurants that seem to be catered only to tourists. Though there are endless sights and museums to see all throughout the city, three main hotspots stick out to me as crawling with tourists: by the Eiffel Tower in the 7th, Montmartre in the 18th, and the Saint-Germain-des-Prés in the 6th. These areas are certainly beautiful and worth a visit, but you will also find restaurants that will charge you 8 euros for a hot chocolate. Maybe the hot chocolate is exceptionally good, but you are mostly paying for the location or the view.

I like to think of these places as the Paris we see in the movies, or a sort of Disneyworld, yet when I actually go there, all I see are tourists. They are beautiful spots to discover and take some photographs, but it's not the place I would go if I want to be the only foreigner drinking a coffee on a terrasse, for example. Everyone has their own experience of Paris and I prefer to go a bit more off the beaten path.

19. WHY DO THE SERVERS HATE US?

There is a stereotype in Paris that people are rude. There is of course some truth in every stereotype, but there are also cultural differences that account for this. When my parents visit Paris from the States, they are under the impression that all the servers in restaurants and cafés hate them. This is usually not the case. When I go back to the United States, I am always taken aback by how friendly the servers are because I've gotten so used to how different the service is in Paris. Americans in general are known to be more outgoing and openly friendly than the French who like to keep to themselves.

There is a major difference between service in Paris and service in the United States: enthusiasm. In Paris, the waiter may not come to your table right away, and they may even throw the menu down and just stare at you, waiting to take your order. I tell my parents that it's nothing personal, it's just the way it is.

Their indifference to you as a customer could just be from the fact that they don't have to work for tips like in the United States. There are cultural differences that explain this behavior. When the

Eat Like a Local

waiter doesn't bring you the check straight away at the end of the meal, it's not because they don't like you. It's because they are usually not in any rush. Once again, the French enjoy their time at the table and aren't trying to run out of the restaurant as soon as the meal is over. They may enjoy an espresso after their dessert or a digestif.

20. TIPS: ARE THEY EXPECTED?

Unlike the United States, in France there is a minimum wage for all service professions that does not make tips an obligation. Servers in France are salaried employees that earn a living wage, get paid vacations, and health care. In the United States, this is not the case. I forgot to tip once in a bar when I was back in the States and got kicked out. Servers have to take their tips seriously in the United States because without them, they don't make a living wage.

Luckily in France, if you forget to tip you certainly won't get kicked out of the establishment! You can tip 5-15% in France if you really appreciate the service and the meal, but it is not necessary. The price you see is the price you get. Tax is also included in the prices that are shown on the menu and on the items in supermarkets, unlike in the United States. I've rarely seen my French friends tip, and it's usually my American friends that are visiting that add a little something extra to the bill. It's a nice gesture but not an obligation.

21. LES BOUILLONS: TRADITIONAL FRENCH FOOD ON A BUDGET

On the top of my list for places to eat traditional French food on a budget in Paris are the Bouillons. The Bouillons are restaurants that began to appear in Paris in the 19th century where the working class would go to eat the food that the Bourgeois didn't want. The prices were low and the portions large, and the ambiance was usually a jovial one. This still rings true today!

Today, there are multiple locations around the city where you can enjoy a boeuf bourguignon and a pitcher of red wine among friends without breaking the bank. In addition to the reasonable prices and traditional French plates, you will enjoy your meal in a magnificent setting of art nouveau decor and be waited on by servers that are all dressed in classy black vests and bowties. It's a great place to celebrate a birthday and if you're lucky, the staff may sing you a song for the occasion.

My favorite traditional dishes at these restaurants include the French onion soup, which is the best I've had in all of Paris, the leek starter, and the classic boeuf bourguignon. After the meal, finish it all off with the famous profiteroles for dessert. Among the various locations, Bouillon Chartier is my favorite for the decor and Bouillon Pigalle for the more modern and youthful vibe. Make sure to get there early as there is usually a line!

22. DATE NIGHT IN BELLEVILLE: DRINKS AND DUMPLINGS

One of my favorite areas of Paris is the Belleville neighborhood spread between the 10th and 20th arrondissements. From the Parc de Belleville you have a great view of the entire city and the surrounding winding streets make this area feel like a little village. There are lots of cute bars and restaurants in the area to choose from, but I will share with you some of my personal favorites for a special date night.

Start off the evening with a cocktail on the terrasse at Les Mesanges and then watch the sunset from the Belvédère in the park. Head on over to the Rue de Belleville to grab a bite to eat. There are many Chinese restaurants in Belleville, but my favorite spot for cheap dumplings is Guo Xin Ravioli. There is always a line out the door because of the delicious plates at reasonable prices. It's a great spot to share an appetizer of sauteed eggplant or napa cabbage followed by a couple plates of grilled dumplings. After dinner, you can continue the evening by having a drink on one of the bustling terrasses in the area like Aux Folies or do some dancing at Café Chéri.

23. THE MAIN PARISIAN CHINATOWN

Though there are multiple areas of Paris with Chinese restaurants and culture, the main Parisian Chinatown is in the 13th arrondissement around the Place d'Italie. You can find lots of good places to eat and Asian grocery stores with products imported directly from China. The most famous one with multiple stores is Tang Freres. They have a large assortment of exotic fruits and vegetables, as well as frozen prepared chinese dishes and a fresh fish market.

I love their dumplings and kimchi and have also tested their tapioca pearls to make my own bubble tea. I'm not an expert on bubble tea however and prefer to enjoy an authentic one made by many of the shops in the area!

24. LITTLE TOKYO: THE JAPANESE QUARTER ON THE RUE SAINTE-ANNE

Craving Japanese food? The Rue Sainte-Anne in the 1st and 2nd arrondissements of Paris is the place to be. Here you can find a wide array of Japanese restaurants, grocery stores, and boulangeries. Enjoy some delicious sushi and ramen at restaurants like Higuma and Happa Te on this street.

Overall, there is a big interest in Japanese culture in France that spans multiple domains, from cuisine to fine arts. You can often find numerous art exhibitions and conferences devoted to Japanese culture in Paris that really highlight this cultural exchange. If you're looking for some literature, there is a great Japanese bookstore in the area called JUNKUDO where you can find manga, beautiful stationery, and lots of books about Japanese culture.

25. MICHELIN STAR RESTAURANTS: TREAT YOURSELF TO CULINARY EXCELLENCE

In 2021, Paris was home to ten Michelin star restaurants each boasting three stars. There are also a handful of one and two star Michelin restaurants that are certainly worth the visit. If you're looking to treat yourself to a decadent tasting menu, try to get a reservation at Chef Alain Passard's three star restaurant Arpège. Other top contenders to delight your taste buds are Guy Savoy in the 6th and Pavillon Ledoyen in the 8th. You are sure to have the ultimate gastronomic experience of the finest dining that Paris has to offer.

26. PUT YOUR TASTE BUDS TO THE TEST

If you're looking for a unique date spot and a reasonably priced tasting menu, check out Pierre Sang's Korean-French fusion restaurant in the 11th arrondissement. With an impressive and reasonably priced dinner menu of 6 courses, you'll enjoy seasonal ingredients that put your taste buds to the test, not to mention their wonderful wine selection. The best part of the experience is that they don't tell you what you're eating before each plate: you have to guess. If you have dietary restrictions or allergies, they make sure to accommodate you.

27. BIG MAMMA: TRADITIONAL ITALIAN TRATTORIAS

Looking for the most delicious pizza in a fun setting? The Big Mamma group has seven different restaurants around Paris where you can enjoy authentic Italian pizzas and fresh pastas in a traditional trattoria setting. The food is delicious and the ambiance is fun, and the servers are usually all Italian. I personally love the decor of these restaurants and always feel like I'm in some sort of Wes Anderson movie when I eat there! My two favorite locations are Popolare in the 2nd and Libertino in the 10th. These are also hotspots that will have lines out the door, so make sure to get there early.

28. LA FELICITA: AN ITALIAN FOOD MARKET AND NIGHTLIFE HOTSPOT

Located in the start-up incubator Station F in the 13th is La Felicita: the large Italian food market and cultural hub of the Big Mamma group. With three different bars, five kitchens, a bakery, and a coffee shop, this spot has it all. In addition to the culinary offerings, La Felicita also hosts concerts, DJ sets, workshops, and even roller disco nights. I went to one of these roller disco nights a couple years ago and absolutely loved it. Check out their website to see the agenda of events for your next date night!

Eat Like a Local

29. GROUND CONTROL: ECLECTIC FOOD HALL

Just across the river from La Felicita in the 12th arrondissement is Ground Control, another cultural hub and food hall. Here you can enjoy a variety of food stands of local and international cuisine while enjoying a pint of artisanal beer amongst friends. They host an eclectic variety of concerts and conferences, as well as vintage fairs and themed festivals. It's a great place to get together with friends on the weekend.

30. TAKE A STROLL THROUGH A FARMER'S MARKET

The most important thing about French cuisine is quality produce. Paris is renowned for its open air farmer's markets where you can find everything you would ever need: seasonal fruits and vegetables, meats and fish, and of course, cheese. Each arrondissement has at least one farmer's market that sets up in the mornings at least two or three fixed days a week and stays open until the early afternoon. You can find a map of these markets and the days they are open in the reference links at the end of this book.

Get to the market early if you want to get your hands on the freshest produce! Some vendors will accept payment by card but most only take cash, so make sure to stop by the ATM ahead of time. Whether planning a picnic in the Luxembourg gardens or cooking a meal at home, the best place to shop is right outside your doorstep.

31. LET'S TALK ABOUT CHEESE

You can't visit Paris without tasting an assortment of French cheeses. Cheese is such an important part of French culture that it has its own course during a meal: it comes after the main course but before the dessert. If you're looking to bring some cheeses to a picnic or a dinner, there are fromageries, or cheese shops, all around the city. Like the famous boulangeries I mentioned early, there is usually one just a 5 minute walk away from anywhere in the city! You can also find good cheese in the supermarkets and the open air markets, but going to a fromagerie is an experience in itself.

Some of the best artisanal fromageries I've been to include Laurent Dubois with four different locations around the city and Chez Virginie in the 18th.

32. THE PROPER ORDER FOR CHEESE TASTING

Once you've found your selection of cheeses to taste, there is one last important step you must take before diving in: determining the order in which you will eat the cheeses. Typically, you are supposed to try the mildest cheeses first, like a goat's cheese, and finish with the ones that are stronger in taste, like a gorgonzola or truffle cheese. It's important to prepare your palette and save the best, or strongest, for last. If you're unsure of which cheeses are the strongest or most aged, don't hesitate to ask.

33. THE BEST PART ABOUT THE HOLIDAYS

The best part about the holidays in France is most definitely the food! The months leading up to Christmas are a festive time where Parisians break out the champagne and foie gras, the hot wine and fondue. A traditional meal to have amongst family or friends during this time is a raclette: melted cheese on potatoes with charcuterie and cornichons on the side. It's quite a heavy meal that usually lasts multiple hours and includes several bottles of wine. It's the type of meal that you eat on a cold and rainy winter evening in Paris with a group of loved ones to celebrate the festive season with.

34. A JANUARY TRADITION: GALETTES DES ROIS

Galettes des rois, or king's cake, is a Christian tradition celebrated in France on January 6th. During this holiday you eat a cake that is made of puff pastry and frangipane but can also be made with fruits. Inside each cake is a fève, a small figurine, and the person who gets the piece with the fève inside gets crowned the king. The cakes are sold with paper crowns in boulangeries and supermarkets to ensure this tradition.

There is a funny tradition about this holiday that I've experienced firsthand: the youngest of the group has to go under the table and name the recipient of each piece of the cake as it is cut. That way there is no way of knowing who will get the fève!

35. LA FÊTE DE LA CHANDELEUR: CELEBRATE WITH CRÊPES

Every year on February 2nd is another Christian tradition that involves food. This time, we eat crêpes! 40 days after the birth of Jesus is his presentation to the temple and this holiday celebrates that occasion. The round form and golden color of crêpes is said to represent the sun and the days that begin to grow longer. We eat crêpes to celebrate the cycle of the seasons and the imminent arrival of the spring! You can enjoy the crêpes with butter and sugar, lemon, or nutella.

36. WINE AND STREET FOOD IN MONTMARTRE: FÊTE DES VENDANGES

In early October, the annual Fête Des Vendanges in Montmartre celebrates the harvesting of grapes to make wine. The festival usually runs for four or five days throughout the little cobblestoned streets next to the Sacré Coeur and includes many stands with local vineyards selling their wine. There are also food stands where you can enjoy everything from oysters to raclette sandwiches. It is usually a very festive occasion where people will spend their Saturday afternoon tasting different wines, listening to live music, and enjoying a day outside in the sun. It has been such a popular event in past years that it usually gets very crowded, so be prepared for large crowds!

Eat Like a Local

37. LATE NIGHT EATS

If you're spending a night out on the town and can't make it to the restaurant before the kitchen closes, there are some late night options in store. Some bistrots stay open late but usually the go to option is getting a kebab. There is a kebab shop on practically every street corner in Paris and it is definitely an authentic experience that is loved by locals!

38. THE BEST FALAFEL IN PARIS

Craving a falafel sandwich? Head on over to the famous hotspot L'As du Fallafel in the 4th arrondissement to enjoy their traditional Isreali cuisine. Make sure you get there early as there are often people waiting in line. If you prefer to get take-out, you can bring your sandwich next door to eat it in the secret garden le Jardin des Rosiers, nestled in the heart of the Marais.

39. HOW DO YOU LIKE YOUR MEAT?

For meat eaters, it is important to know the French words for how you like your meat cooked. From my experience, the French prefer their meat on the rare side and are fans of everything that is tartare, or raw, so it's good to learn some simple vocabulary to make sure the piece of meat you ordered comes out as you like it.

After you order your dish, the server will ask you about "la cuisson", or the cooking. There are multiple ways you can respond. "Bleu" is the term for meat cooked on a very hot grill for one minute on each side. Next up is "saignant" which literally translates to "bloody" and means rare. "À point" is the equivalent of medium-rare and "bien cuit" is well-cooked. Now you can order your meal with confidence!

40. CERTAIN MEATS CAN BE ROSÉ AND THEY SHOULD BE

Another cooking term that can be confusing if you're not a native speaker is "rosé". When I was at a restaurant and the server asked me if I wanted my lamb "rosé", I thought he was offering me a glass of rosé wine with my meal. Of course I said yes. After he awkwardly had to explain that he was referring to the cooking, I said I would prefer the lamb "bien cuit". Rosé is somewhere between rare and well-cooked and I prefer my meat more cooked than raw. Apparently I offended the server because in his mind, and in French cuisine, lamb is supposed to be eaten rosé as it is the best expression of the meat. If you would like to eat your meat as the chef would typically prepare it but are unsure of the cooking, you can ask.

41. CULINARY FAUX-PAS: WHAT TO BE CAREFUL OF

In addition to my experience of ordering the "wrong version" of lamb, there have been other occasions at a French dinner table where a simple action was subtly offensive. For example, I've learned not to add salt or pepper, or any other spices or sauces for that matter, to my meal before I've tasted it. It can be offensive to the chef if you add other ingredients to their dish before you've even tried it.

Another small but important detail of respecting the cuisine is about what you leave on your plate. I've noticed that in the United States there is a lot more of a focus on consumption and in turn, a lot more waste. The French do not like anything to go to waste, and if you leave food on your plate it usually sends the message that you did not enjoy the meal because you didn't finish it. Of course these rules are not set in stone anywhere, but I wish I had known them before getting myself into some awkward situations.

42. SIMPLICITY, SIMPLICITY, SIMPLICITY

One overarching factor that I appreciate about French cuisine is simplicity. In the United States, there is often a belief that bigger is better and that combining all the ingredients imaginable will make for a delicious meal. This is the total opposite of French cuisine, which is focused on less is more and letting individual flavors shine through rather than combining too many things together.

There is an attention to detail and also to the quality of the ingredients you choose to combine. A French friend of mine asked me about peanut butter and jelly sandwiches, an American staple, with a confused and shocked look on his face, saying, "Peanut butter is sweet, jelly is sweet, why are you mixing two sweet things together like that? It's too much sweet!" I personally love a good peanut butter and jelly sandwich but it's true that from a French perspective, this combination is considered sacrilege.

43. THE BEST SPOTS FOR MEXICAN FOOD

After growing up in the United States and being spoiled with Mexican food, I knew I would be craving some tacos while living in Paris. Don't be fooled by the fast food chain "O'Tacos" as they serve what are known as "French tacos" and do not resemble anything close to Mexican style tacos. You can see for yourself but if you have any expectations like I did, you will leave confused and potentially disappointed. The best spots in the city for an authentic experience are El Nopal in the 9th and 10th and Anahuacalli in the 5th.

44. MOSQUÉE DE PARIS: TAGINES, PASTRIES AND MINT TEA

One of my favorite places to eat in Paris is the Grand Mosque in the 5th arrondissement. They have delicious tagines with couscous and oriental pastries, all in the beautiful setting of blue mosaics that seem to transport you to Morocco. Enjoy a sweet mint tea in the courtyard surrounded by plants and little birds chirping in the trees. For ladies only, you can spend a couple hours relaxing in the all-female hammam and receiving a traditional gommage and massage.

45. A MEAL ON THE HOUSE

It seems crazy to think that you could eat a meal without taking out your wallet in Paris, but you can! This is an insider tip that I learned directly from the locals. A couple different cafés around the city offer free meals on certain nights of the week for their clients.

On Wednesdays, Le Bouillon Belge in the 20th offers a free plate of mussels after 5pm. On Thursdays, you can eat merguez sausages and couscous at Les Trois Frères in the 18th for the price of one drink. On Friday and Saturday evening, you can enjoy free couscous at the Tribal Café in the 10th and Le Grenier in the 11th.

Eat Like a Local

46. TASTE THE FAMOUS ICE CREAM AT BERTHILLON

For those with a sweet tooth, Berthillon ice cream shop on the Île Saint-Louis is the place to be. Berthillon is world renowned for its luxury ice cream and sorbets made from only natural ingredients and offering over 70 flavors. They also have a tea room with a decadent assortment of pastries to choose from. Get there early to beat the line and enjoy your ice cream while sitting on the banks of the Seine!

47. WHERE TO MAKE RESERVATIONS AND FIND NEW INSIDER HOTSPOTS

Looking to book a reservation for the new insider hotspots in town? Find restaurants and book online through the application The Fork. There are often restaurants with deals and discounts if you book through the application. Another good reference point for finding new hip restaurants is Le Fooding. They are the reference point for scoping out the new neo-bistros and cool fusion restaurants in the city.

48. BEST BURGER JOINTS

At most Parisian bistros you can find a good burger, but there are also a couple great restaurants that are centered around gourmet burgers and do a pretty good job at it. The top two burger establishments on my list with multiple locations around the city are PNY and Le Camion Qui Fume. Don't forget the fries on the side!

49. ARTISANAL COFFEE ROASTERS

Parisians usually drink their coffee in the form of an espresso or allongé, or long espresso, but there are more and more artisanal coffee roasters popping up around the city that propose more options. As an American, I often crave a good drip coffee or iced coffee.

For a good hot brew or latte, try KB Coffee Roasters in the 9th or Coutume located in the Finland Institute in the 5th. For a delicious iced coffee to cool down in the summer months, head on over to Partisan Café Artisanal in the 3rd.

50. LET YOUR TASTE BUDS LEAD THE WAY

Paris has endless opportunities when it comes to exploring new flavors and cuisines. The most important thing to remember when navigating the food scene is to keep an open mind and try to see the entire experience from a different perspective than your own. What I love about French cuisine is the pride that goes along with sourcing quality ingredients and the attention to detail of individual flavors. To come to a foreign table and eat is to be introduced to a new culture, and I encourage you to do so with open arms.

BONUS TIPS

Apart from the amazing food culture in Paris, I'd love to share some bonus tips with you about some of my favorite aspects of the city! These bonus tips are just the icing on the cake to really get you thinking like a local and take advantage of the time you spend in Paris.

When I first arrived, I was so motivated to go to every single place in the guidebooks and test out all the cool bars and restaurants. I have been here for five years now and can honestly say that I still haven't seen it all! I've come to appreciate finding my own routines of where I spend my time in the city and making my own memories, and I hope you will too. To give you a head start, here is the inside scoop on cocktails, music venues, museums, and day trips that may inspire you to call Paris your home one day too.

51. THE BEST COCKTAIL BARS IN PARIS

There are so many options to choose from when it comes to finding a good cocktail bar in Paris. Every year, there is even a cocktail festival that lasts a week and is devoted to the craft of mixology and promoting the newest hotspots in the city. During this week you can enjoy special deals and attend cocktail events and workshops. I have a list of my favorite spots that can be enjoyed all year round where you can go for an intimate date night or amongst friends.

If you're looking for a cocktail bar to transport you to a tropical getaway, check out Dirty Dick in the 9th. Just next door is Lulu White, a classy and more upscale spot to test some old-fashioned cocktails. For a cocktail bar that plays smooth grooves on exclusively vinyl, check out Fréquence in the 11th. If you want a fancy evening out on the town, head on over to Bar Hemingway at the Ritz in the 1st.

52. DID SOMEONE SAY SPEAKEASY?

I've always loved the idea of going to a speakeasy: going through some back door to find a secret entrance to a hidden bar. These spots usually borrow decor from the prohibition era of the 1920s and can really transport you back in time. There are numerous speakeasies throughout Paris but some personal favorites come to mind.

Hidden inside of a laundromat in the 11th is Lavomatic, a quirky speakeasy with inventive cocktails. La Mezcaleria hidden behind the kitchen of the Hotel 1K in the 3rd has the largest collection of mezcal in Paris and also serves delicious South-American tapas. Voted one of the 50 best bars in the world in 2017 is the Little Red Door speakeasy in the 3rd. Here you can enjoy modern cocktails in a cozy and exclusive setting.

53. TAKE IN THE VIEWS ON A ROOFTOP BAR

One of the most beautiful things about Paris is it's skyline: the Eiffel tower sparkling across the river from the Sacré Coeur on the hill in Montmartre, with the charming rooftops and little chimneys in between. To take in the view and enjoy a drink at the same time, there are some great rooftop bars to choose from.

Watch the Eiffel tower glisten at night from Le Perchoir rooftop bar, with locations in the 11th, 4th, and 15th arrondissements. For a youthful and trendy atmosphere and a great view of Sacré Coeur, check out Khayma Rooftop at Generator in the 10th. If you want to experience an evening at a luxury champagne bar and restaurant, La Terrasse at the Hôtel Raphael in the 16th is for you.

Eat Like a Local

54. WHERE TO LISTEN TO LIVE JAZZ

As a musician, I've gotten to know a lot about the venues in Paris and gotten to play at many of them! The Paris music scene is eclectic and there is live music usually every night of the week.

If you are looking to listen to some jazz, there are many great places you can go. For a typical left bank experience listening to a traditional jazz trio in a stone "cave", or basement, check out Caveau de la Huchette in the 5th. Le Baiser Salé across the river in the 1st also has great live jazz shows that incorporate afro and fusion influences. La Gare in the 19th located in an old train station is more of an underground jazz venue with a younger crowd and eclectic agenda.

55. THE HOTSPOTS FOR POP, ROCK, AND INDIE CONCERTS

There are some great venues for pop, rock and indie concerts from French bands and international acts. Le Pop Up du Label in the 12th is a fun spot to discover new up and coming artists on the indie scene. Also in the 12th, Supersonic is known for showcasing different rock bands every night of the week and finishing the evening with some vintage 70s music DJ sets. I recently played a show on the traditional Chinese 3 masted wooden boat, La Dame de Canton, on the quai of the Seine in the 13th. They have been hosting weekly gigs where you can discover three different bands in one night and enjoy a meal in their restaurant below deck before the show. La Boule Noire in the 9th and Point Ephemere in the 10th are also some of my favorite venues to catch a show.

Eat Like a Local

56. MUSEUM MUST-SEES

In May 2019, Paris was named the museum capital of the world, boasting 297 museums in total. The Louvre is by far the most visited museum in the world and is home to many famous works of art, including Da Vinci's Mona Lisa. As someone who is not a fan of long lines and crowded places, I didn't dare visit the Louvre until recently. When the museums reopened during the pandemic but there weren't many tourists, I took the opportunity to spend the afternoon there and was pleased to have the place mostly to myself. The Louvre is definitely a must see on the museum list, but be prepared for large crowds or try to time your visit in the off-season. Also, it's important to know that the Louvre has a very extensive collection of art that cannot be seen in just one day.

If you love impressionist paintings and consider yourself a romantic, the Musée d'Orsay in the 7th and the Musée de l'Orangerie in the 1st are for you. I personally could spend hours getting lost in Monet's large water lily canvasses at the l'Orangerie and then blissfully stroll through the Jardin des Tuileries.

For lovers of modern and contemporary art, the Centre Pompidou in the 4th is the place to be. The

Palais de Tokyo and the Fondation Louis Vuitton, both located in the 16th, are also wonderful museums with thought provoking exhibits and events.

57. HIDDEN TREASURES

Paris has some wonderful small museums that are a bit more off the beaten path but are well worth a visit. Among my favorites are the Musée de la Vie romantique in the 9th and the Musée de Montmartre in the 18th. Both of these quaint museums have cafés where you can enjoy a cup of tea in a charming courtyard garden.

The Grande Galerie de l'Évolution, or the natural history museum, is also a great museum for the whole family. Located in the Jardin des Plantes in the 5th arrondissement, this museum celebrates biodiversity with it's large collection of taxidermy animals and specimens.

58. STROLL THROUGH MONET'S GARDENS IN GIVERNY

Paris has so much to offer inside of its borders, but if you're craving a little day trip or weekend getaway to the countryside, there are a handful of great locations just a short train ride away. Just an hour outside of the city are the lush gardens and home of painter Claude Monet in Giverny. The French impressionist painter lived in Giverny for 43 years and many of his most famous paintings, including his water lilies, were painted here.

Monet's house and gardens are open to the public from late spring until the fall during the peak season when everything is in bloom. As a florist myself, I love bringing my bike on the train and taking a ride through the countryside to visit the gardens in springtime. For any artists or lovers of nature, this is the perfect day trip for you.

59. GET OFF THE BEATEN PATH TO THE MEDIEVAL TOWN OF PROVINS

If you're looking for a day trip that goes back a bit further in time, check out the medieval town of Provins. This town is a UNESCO world heritage site and boasts beautiful architecture and small winding cobblestoned streets that will charm you. My partner and I took a day trip to Provins during their annual medieval festival, which is the biggest in France, and tasted some traditional medieval treats, watched parade goers in medieval costume, and enjoyed hot wine from a cauldron. It was a very unique experience that I would highly recommend for anyone who loves traditional festivals and being transported back in time!

60. LIVE LIKE THE KING AND QUEEN FOR A DAY IN VERSAILLES

The most popular day trip from Paris is definitely Versailles, and it is certainly worth the visit. The extravagance of the château and gardens are really a sight to see and are a paradise for any French history buffs or lovers of baroque architecture. Make sure to check out the famous Hall of Mirrors in the château and the beautiful Rococo ceiling in the queen's bedroom. The grounds are quite expansive, so if you are courageous you can go by foot, but the best way to discover Versailles is definitely by bike.

When I visited Versailles with my family we rented bikes that we brought on the train from Paris. You can also rent bikes directly in Versailles as well. When we arrived at the train station, we biked over to the farmer's market to shop for some fresh produce before heading over to the grounds for a picnic. We were then able to visit the château and gardens, bike back to the station, and be back in Paris in time for dinner!

OTHER RESOURCES:

Map of Farmer's Markets: https://www.paris.fr/pages/les-marches-parisiens-2428

The Fork: https://www.thefork.com/

Le Fooding: https://lefooding.com/en

READ OTHER BOOKS BY CZYK PUBLISHING

Eat Like a Local United States Cities & Towns

Eat Like a Local United States

Eat Like a Local- Oklahoma: Oklahoma Food Guide

Eat Like a Local- North Carolina: North Carolina Food Guide

Eat Like a Local- New York City: New York City Food Guide

Children's Book: Charlie the Cavalier Travels the World by Lisa Rusczyk

Eat Like a Local

Follow *Eat Like a Local* on Amazon.
Join our mailing list for new books

http://bit.ly/EatLikeaLocalbooks

CZYKPublishing.com

Made in United States
North Haven, CT
07 December 2022